TRAVERSE

TRAVERSE

GEORGE ELLIOTT CLARKE

EXILE
editions

Fiction, Poetry, Translation, Drama and Nonfiction

Library and Archives Canada Cataloguing in Publication

Clarke, George Elliott, 1960-, author
        Traverse / George Elliott Clarke.

Poems.
Issued in print and electronic formats.
ISBN 978-1-55096-395-3 (pbk.) — ISBN 978-1-55096-396-0 (pdf)

  I. Title.

PS8555.L3748T73 2014   C811'.54   C2014-900184-3
                                            C2014-900185-1

Design and Composition by Mishi Uroboros.
Typeset in Bodoni SvtyTwo, Constantia, Cochin and Trajan fonts at the Moons of
  Jupiter Studios.

Published by Exile Editions Ltd ~ www.ExileEditions.com
144483 Southgate Road 14 – GD, Holstein, Ontario, N0G 2A0
Printed and Bound in Canada in 2014, by Imprimerie Gauvin

We gratefully acknowledge the Canada Council for the Arts, the Government of Canada
through the Canada Book Fund (CBF), the Ontario Arts Council, and the Ontario
Media Development Corporation, for their support toward our publishing activities.

Canadian Sales: The Canadian Manda Group, 165 Dufferin Street,
Toronto ON M6K 3H6 www.mandagroup.com 416 516 0911

North American and International Distribution, and U.S. Sales:
Independent Publishers Group, 814 North Franklin Street,
Chicago IL 60610 www.ipgbook.com toll free: 1 800 888 4741

for
Geraldine Elizabeth Clarke
(1939 – 2000)
&
William Lloyd Clarke
(1935 – 2005)

African Baptists, Adepts, Believers.

CROSSING

The salt-wavy tumult traverse alone.
—EZRA POUND

But I
had been falling for thirty years.
—ROBIN SKELTON

PREFACE

Anniversaries revivify: They justify indulgences, eccentricities, luxuries, and mercies. My private calendar is not as rich with reverent observances as others' may be, but I do grant select dates transcendent import. See July 1st. True: Canada Day salutes the Dominion's birth as a British Royal-loyal state constituted to deny the United States absolute suzerainty over this continent. But this date is pivotal personally, for, it was on July 1, 1975, in Halifax, Nova Scotia, that I inked several "songs" – as a 15-year-old – and began my apprenticeship to the art of poetry. Thirty years later, at age 45, I decided to review my being and doings as a poet. So, on July 1, 2005, while visiting Halifax, I drafted a verse-memoir to canvass my vital inspirations and the cobbling of my works up to then. What emerged was a series of "Rap Sonnets" – poems to be read aloud. The initial title was direct: *Thirty Years (1975-2005)*. In 2006, I began to publish the poem's sonnet-stanzas, in numerical/chronological sequence, in journals: *ARC*, *Echolocation*, *For Crying Out Loud*, *ELQ/ Exile the Literary Quarterly*. (I thank the editors of these publications for their support.) *ELQ/Exile* has taken most of the "sonnets," and so more than half of this book has appeared in print since 2006. Assuredly, *ELQ/Exile* has liked the poem(s) enough to propose that the work outright now appear under its related imprint, Exile Editions. To aid that purpose, I've re-envisioned my title to *Traverse*, a word pleasingly both a verb and a noun. So, I conceive this book as both recording a portage *and* remarking a bridge. I have added here a closing nonet of "Rap Sonnets," to catalogue events and publications since July 1, 2005. For those who rue the loss of the original "Thirty Year" rubric, I'll note that 2013 marks thirty years since my first book of poetry appeared, i.e., *Saltwater Spirituals and Deeper Blues*, on yet another paramount date, namely, June 6th.

Though *Traverse* is autobiographical, I have manumitted some names and omitted others. I have also overlooked many signal moments such as my debut tour, in April 1977, to Church Point, Nova Scotia (where I viewed snow flurries round a lighthouse); my Fall 1981 residence in a Toronto subway station; my April 1993 encirclement by gun-hefting border guards at Port Huron, Michigan (where my entry to the U.S. "to give a talk on poetry" inspired alarm); my surf-side, noon-sun mugging by three thugs in Salvador, Brazil, in November 2007; and my receipt of The Queen's inadvertently deferential nod in Halifax in June 2010 (She mistook me for a cleric: A reasonable error, given my surname.) Nor have I elaborated (or belaboured) my poetics: "Canadian" by origin, but "African" by inclination. Thus, like Canuck poets, I dignify; like Black poets, I signify.

George Elliott Clarke
Cambridge, Massachusetts
25/12/13

Saltwater Spirituals. Eds. Ronald Tetreault and the class members of English 4010. 23 April 2002. Dalhousie University Electronic Text Centre. http://etc.dal.ca/clarke/index_std.html.

** My radical pedagogues—those who taught me how to analyze and question when I was aged 16 to 19—were Jacqueline Barkley, Walter Borden, Carol Gibbons, Bev Greenlaw, Sylvia Hamilton, Fred Holtz, Joan Jones, Rocky Jones, and Terry Symonds. All once-Haligonians, they composed an open-door avant-garde, an open-sesame intelligentsia.

Scan the QR to enjoy a video of George Elliott Clarke speaking about
the book: he looks back to the moment it came into being,
on one day, July 1, 1985, marking 30 years of his writing poetry.

Or access via URL at: www.tinyurl.com/ClarkeTraverse

(8:44)

DA CAPO: 1 /7/75*

...the beautiful seems right
By force of beauty....
                    —Elizabeth Barrett Browning

---

*Cf. "Poetry: 1/7/75 — 1/7/05" in *Black* (2006) and "July 1, 1975" in *I & I* (2009).

I

What was handed down
    was backtalk—
"nasty Nofaskoshan" noise—
    black and insolent,
an A-to-Z menagerie
    of braying—or caterwauling—script,
"cryin out loud" cryptic adorations—
    Christ and *curry* and *queynte*,
not only in that order—
    via a hodgepodge of fountain pens,
one quixotic, the rest antique,
    straggling ink between wispy
lines, letting letters light,
    dead-on, biting into paper.

II

Under black—but blazing—eyes,
    I ruled pages, slant-wise,
because, wayward as a Goliard,
    I thought kazoos could serenade bulldozers,
or that gold could sun rain.
    I thought I could import Storyville
to a ghetto of fiddles and bagpipes, eh?
    I was tryin to graduate
from grape *Kool-Aid* to *Manischewitz* wine,
    from illegible crayons
to illegitimate poems,
    to go howling after white vamps with black hearts,
and glean hot perfumes from their arctic flesh
    off-and-on any sweaty sofa.

III

Upon a domain of *Gravitas*, I trespassed,
    that beginner's Dominion Day, falling,
where rude books made bodies plain,
    spread-eagling *Love*,
affixing her—*sorta*—to a crucifix.
    Lyrics turned as dark as the innards
of radios, stench of ozone accenting
    cat-piss smells of LP jackets.
Their genius gave me chills
    and made me want to throw up—
as if reading were the same experience
    as watching a piano explode.
Damned be witless *Abstraction*, gutless *Dreams*,
    heartless *Ideals*!

IV

My pitched ears slurped up *Music*'s juices;
  mine eyes gobbled gilt wine plus *hors d'oeuvres*—
the *Champagne*-and-caviar look of each page.
  Anthologies were subversive—half-Tijuana bible
and half-marijuana dream:
  Here's *sado-maso* Poe diddling Plath;
there's slave-tradin Rimbaud buggering Verlaine.
  And, like some *Lumpen* Black Panther or Vandal,
I ransacked New Directions Pound,
  Faber T.S. Eliot, City Lights Ginsberg,
McClelland & Stewart Leonard Cohen,
  Penguin Books Baudelaire,
Farrar, Strauss, Giroux Walcott,
  and Third World Press Carolyn M. Rodgers.[*]

------

[*]Cf. Amiri Baraka.

V

(I ain't forgotten Henry Dumas, Conrad Kent Rivers,
    Robert Hayden, or Jean Toomer.
I don't shun their Deep South sermons,
    their Harlemonious harmonies.
Their pages unfurl as thin as moonshine.
    You tip one of their Gypsy poems,
and it tips you over, tipsy.
    Their words float just like Mary Poppins—
but sting just like Muhammad Ali.
    Suddenly, Queen Elizabeth's English
turns Negroid, Mongoloid, dawdling,
    and lavish in the mouth.
Now, you know "to draw down poems" means tappin
    born-again, now deathless trees.)

VI

I was reading way too much.

    My eyes were as bad as my manners;
my manners were as bad as my speech.

    Literature set me a-stutter
cos ma black tongue could ne'er sound learnèd.

    Sounded more like (a) foul play.
I mean, I was unsound. Dig?

    My Marxism-Leninism enlisted
Pushkin, Pasternak, Rasputin,

    plus Nabokov's *Lolita*.
My Maoism mixed sake and haiku

    et les bons mots de Pierre Elliott Trudeau.
But Irving Layton modelled a swaggering guru:

    "Take down a gal. *Get taken down* by a gal."

VII

Them days, I navigated Halifax like a three-leggèd cat,
    alert but hurt, limping,
moanin open-heart-surgery blues—
    facin the stink of bad news,
slop of bad shots, sobs of liquor,
    while syringes stretched buddies on ice,
cold as burnt-out fire hydrants;*
    and parading tarts made their privates
public for a price—
    never too much. I only wanted
to make love when the moon gleamed sunny,
    white chicks looked coloured, and ink
streamed from me, fluorescent,
    blossoming luminous....

---

*Spotted in Detroit, Michigan, where I was an ACORN agent, in February
1982.

VIII

Didn't I freeze, perambulating frozen,
    peninsular Halifax,
North End to South End to North,
    crossing and double-crossing *Hierarchy*
and *Caste* and *Race* and *Sex*,
    stumblin at times them fault-lines?
As intoxicated as Lear, I staggered raggedly,
    takin blows of rain and snow,
or slaps of rain and snow and tears,
    stinging my black face breathless.
Fog and snow and rain and tears....
    Store windows spit neon to bleach me white.
My genes were impure,
    my blue jeans were dirty.

IX

Once I penetrated the oval, cuntal Legislature,
    where he drove his fist into his seat, that teacher,
excited by N.S. Question Period hysterics—
    orgasms of elect, silk-suited bawds
and taxpayer-bankrolled gamblers—
    stunted members snapped in sheets—
beds, cash, tabloids, and then postage stamps
    (after their scandals kindle, then pall,
leaving only ashen, blurry rumour).
    Amazing it was to stand outlaw in the womb
of *Law*, inside a Palladian-style parliament,
    so near the lawless, unruly Atlantic,
its waves always rearin to erase
    deeds—and even the memory of deeds.

X

YHZ always was tearin
    to go topsy-turvy.
I fantasized each street turned upside-down—
    dunked deep underwater—
as if a perverted Atlantis, or an *Earthquake* version
    of Paul Gallico's *Poseidon Adventure.*
Every tavern radiated rebellion—
    the demented glory of overflowing beer pitchers.
I held ideas as if holding a party,
    stood sunflowers on the North End Library rooftop,
lifted French from records voicing suspicions,
    and eyed James Brown vaulting from vinyl
like light ricocheting off a gold brick.
    But soon *Love* had me all upside-down.

XI

But how could I woo second-cousin Nona—
  no-plain-face Muse, outta Three Mile Plains?
(Neither miles of small print nor the sprawl of epic
  can image her *Majesty*.)
My relation, never true love, nevertheless, her smile
  mimed *Mona Lisa* elusiveness;
her *Négritude*, camouflaged, tinted her skin
  a hint of New Orleans pralines;
her kiss had—I had to guess—the savour
  of honeyed milk.
Her romances were always capital-R *Romantic*.
  Her jokes were as earnest as Romero's Zombies.
Her 45s reeled card-table, 60-watt gloom
  and auto-wreck, 60 m.p.h. pain.

XII

Hangin out, lingering, with Nona,
    I got cultured in pickles, guitars, car engines.
She cared less about doing well for herself
    than doing good for others.
I could spy the legacy of *Slavery*
    divulged poignantly in our very colours—
blue-green-grey eyes or molasses ones,
    blond(e) or copper or black hair
(that was either rambunctiously curly
    or pass-for-white straight).
The consequence of my unsolicited
    and quite unsophisticated desire
was to watch blushing roses blossom
    and taste them in apple pie.

XIII

Forgive, please, these down-home metaphors,
    but Nona was like a horse
I couldn't ride, couldn't even pet,
    but for whom I was secretly giddy—
likely enough to plunge over cliffs.
    Thus, my first love mirrored her blondeness.
(O, Nona, how could you have shot yourself,
    and emptied out all your irreplaceable blood,
and blasted your gorgeous being, never vulgar,
    into the soulless solace of a casket?)
That premier girl's initials are O.K.
    Okay? She was a premium knockout.
How could I not feel kayoed
    by that svelte and vexing intellectual?

XIV

An Acadian *fille* with a foxy, Okie name,
    only clandestinely English,
she urged me to be primal, musky, moody,
    while she swallowed the Eucharistic pill.
But my eyes and ears weren't yet open,
    not yet truly formed.
My blood had still to pump
    like a shotgun,
to charge—or discharge—the lusts tussling
    in my cranium's Coliseum.
I thought I could return the sunken *Titanic*
    to its pristine blueprints, I mean,
get back to Eden. But my shaky theories sabotaged
    our wham-bam, shindig shebang.

XV

I dubbed that stubby, chubby, fedora'd fogey,
     hoggin the corner of Maynard and Cunard,
a stogie boogyin in his choppers,
     "The Dictator of Guff"—
that actual roller of shit-smell cigars—
     as if he were the Chairman
of funereal, unreal, Bluenose Halifax.
     Split-secondly, O. evolved into "Layla"—
Aury's O (as drawn by Derek and the Dominoes)—
     and erased me like obscene, sidewalk chalk.
What else could I do,
   but go underground,
mine authentic B.B. King howls,
     undermine my M.L. King dreams?

XVI

I went down into my Aunt's house, "Big Grey"
    (named to honour The Band's Big Pink,
the house that begat *The Basement Tapes*,
    Dylan's Nobel Prize album), above the charcoal harbour,
and bid an Underwood 315 cloacal typewriter
    replace a real-gone girlfriend,
her spectral, holy eyes burning
    holes in my haunted sonnets.
Typewriter keys croaked crookedly,
    spewing pages askew with garbage feelings,
Country-n-Western stupidity, because ...
    I couldn't admit O. had trashed—
dumped, dismissed, and dashed—
    me like an anorexic Buddha.

XVII

Zigzagged I cross that niggardly no-man's-land
    of no-woman.
Cooped up in an odious cave—
    that basement, quivering with cockroaches—
I had to don reflective sunglasses
    so I'd not reflect on my *Jōvan Musk* tears.
I couldn't box my way
    out the stocks I was in,
and the clacking typewriter rounded that fact,
    orbited the pain,
by locking, into their serial place,
    imprints of cast-metal letters
that nailed down every vision
    ink and drink brought up.

XVIII

I felt "Down and Out" without
    ever having risen
from the catacomb's dim damp—
    those tearful aches, beatific pangs—
lusts purpled and steeped in Concorde wine,
    or dyed blue by T & A mags.
I hustled an escape—like Houdini
    or Eldridge Cleaver or Ovid,
to neither be ungodly nor satanic,
    but adverse in verse alone.
Whited out by burgundy-black wine,
    my nerves off-key
(like my typewriter keys), I chose to toodle-loo
    to Waterloo to seek a "Victory."

XIX

Shortly, I dallied, delayed, with Suzette,
    Mahogany doll who was smokin,
I mean, searing, smouldering, who made love
    day-long, night-long, and unpocketed
silver-cased, tobacco cancer-sticks,
    and lounged in silver, polyester panties,
and dollied in my lap while I typed (or tried),
    jubilant in a brand-new grotto.
Suzette took up *Huckleberry Finn* and downed
    Tia Maria pon *Tia Maria,*
and mailed letters postmarked from a town
    in the bucolic, ass-fucking Annapolis Valley,
callin out *Love.* Then, she grabbed me and dabbed a goodbye,
    when I nabbed that night train to Ontari-ari-ari-o.

XX

(On her birthday, her virginal sixteenth, precisely,
    Neanderthal yokels had coaxed her
jokingly into their *Coke*-and-rum camp,
    then spliced her, each one, twice each.
A K.K.K. *Rape*: They'd been stalking, frothing.
    The young, dirty wolves would grunt;
the old dogs would just drool, dreamy.
    Then they dragged her down, broke her:
They copied their cutthroat throwbacks
    who'd miscegenated "Negress" slaves.
Suze vented this nausea twixt cigarette-blue breaths
    and tears and gulps of *Tia Maria*.
I had to get away from Nova Scotia,
    not from her, but from Nova Scotia.)

XXI

To Waterloo I shipped, shelving a gangrenous heart,
    to now besiege the *Canon*'s heavyweights—
Chaucer, Shakespeare, Milton, Hopkins, Yeats—
    and smash a train through their fortress.
I used to go nights and stand beside Lake Columbia,
    letting the wind splash those shallow waves
high enough to baptize me with a false image
    of the Atlantic.
Or strolled I always along Laurel Creek,
    planning to elegize Monsignor Moses Coady
and be that black-and-red plaid-shirt, Baptist Marxist—
    to wield the hammer-and-sickle *and* crucifix.
I declared myself now "Nattt Moziah Shaka!"*
    Riled, a pink-faced Tory thrust five pinkies gainst my face.

---

*Cf. Nat Turner (1800-31); Marcus Mosiah Garvey (1887-1940), and Shaka Zulu (1787-1828).

XXII

Wasn't I ridiculous? Sho, I was ridiculous!
High-steppin in crayon shoes and high-hat Afro,
Ogled I a tall, thin, tan, and tantalizin, bo'n Jamaican,
with streaming *noir* hair, dove breasts,
occupying that hallway in Modern Languages,
in her blue-jean skirt and *Ilsa-She-Wolf* black boots.
I deemed her a dazzlingly sable Venus,
rising from demure, but glossy waves,
and she—unlike some Ipanema gal—purred hello
when I wafted her my welcome.
Miracle! She materialized in three classes, Fall 1980,
this earthy, divine Miss H.,
as pretty as Easter lilies,
as pure as lilies in April rain.

XXIII

Yep, she was as Pentecostal as Easter:
   Her fire-branded lips were instantly randy,
carnivorous to bolt plush, plump kisses.
   Though her *Ideals* magazine shivered
my erected *Penthouse*,
   the apple blossoms we angled beneath
were non-judgmental, perfumed, secular,
   serenading *Nature*'s catholic sexuality,
even on the emerald banks of Laurel Creek,
   with its black, Shakespearean swans
and white, Blakean ones,
   or in the weekend-emptied, suburban bungalow
where I had a room and no scruples,
   and she joked I imagined her "barefoot and pregnant"!

XXIV

I bade us execute what we could prosecute,
    negotiating railway mix-ups,
classroom metaphysics, missed-bus fiascoes,
    church non-attendance,
her odyssey by VIA to Ville de Québec,
    my "Long March" hitch-hiking to Vancouver—
all the way from Barrie,
    trembling all night in freezing dew,
or thirsty on the Prairies, swallowing litres of o.j.,
    slogging kilometers that were umpteen miles long,
snapping pics, thumbing rides, praying, writing,
    hungry, wolfing wild blackberries,
swatting mosquitoes, getting shat on by gulls,
    then kiting from Vancouver straight to her bed in Québec.

XXV

Madelle "Ash" opened to me Ramparts, not her own.
      Sir *Justice* opened to us Le Château Frontenac.
We forked caribou; spooned *crème brûlée*; swooned:
      my crayon Sis Corita poster got all crumpled up.
Trembling, I embraced the waist of that wraith,
      and unlaced her wraps. *Faith* collapsed;
we lapsed; and I had to exit Sainte Foy,
      leaving *Mamzelle à* l'Université Laval,
and to attentions and intentions of Afro'd Alpha.

      Thus, I pissed myself weeping back to Waterloo,
then slipped into still-hippy Integrated Studies,
      governed by Dr. De'Ath, cosmo anthropologist,
who, thanks to his studies in Maori New Zealand,
      espied—at once—my Black New Scotland roots.

XXVI

Baptist, but funky, Miz H. illuminated *Beauty*.
    So illogical was I, I was pathological.
She was a trampling gazelle.
    I was a trampled-under gazette.
We blossomed with "Being With You"
    (Smokey Robinson—1981),
but withered into "I Can't Go for That"
    (Hall and Oates—1981).
Damn! Our deep-black Motown Soul
    bleached into blue-eyed Soul—
the *Spirit* sunk back into matter.
    Every blues ballad stuck me deeper in Hell.
Nights, I snuck into the old Hogtown City Morgue
    to punctuate my woes on an I.B.M. *Selectric*.

XXVII

Stealthily, but brazenly, I stole the plum Poli Sci job
    for undergrads, though CBC Radio X'd me
cause I came late to a Current Affairs exam
    I nailed—
explaining the ins-and-outs of Parliament
    and all the Parties and players
in five minutes, *not* the thirty given the white-bread, *et al.*
    So, I vamoosed to Queen's Park,
and the Ontario Elections Commission,
    and thrived, easterly, in the tide-sodden Beaches,
and etched an electoral history of the Constituency
    of Algoma-Manitoulin.
(Maybe it's still there, decidedly dusty,
    on a back shelf—musty—of the Legislative Library.)

XXVIII

Ontario Liberals—*da* "Grits," under then-dorky,
 not yet contact-lens-*chic*, Peterson,
readied me an intern cell (well-padded).
 But I fled the Provincial Parliament
(ochre architecture plagiarizing a Hindu temple),
 sick of seeing Rhodes Scholar Socialist flinch each time my black face
surprised him in a stairwell.
 I dieseled back to Halifax, dieseled back to O.,
to resurrect our ephemeral, teen-age intimacy,
 with candles, Joan Armatrading acoustics,
Pusser's Navy Rum, ideas of Egypt, and high-jinx—
 plus nostalgia for our adolescent gymnastics.
Yet, too soon bore I to Tunnel Mountain, to study, again,
 how I was supposed to imagine *this stuff*....

XXIX

Learned I can't muffle my cantankerous, blues Muse!
    I autographed *Saltwater Spirituals and Deeper Blues*,
while *Madelle* "Ash" sashayed taut hips to Ottawa
    to score a Bachelor in *Kindergarten* tutoring.
Now enduring solo, torturous, redoubled yearning,
    strayed I to Y.Z., Hong Kong Buddhist,
who abided with me while I helmed
    a psychedelic, sex-savvy, crypto-Plato tabloid,
Imprint: student organ of the University of Waterloo.
    Y. boiled bok choy, tolerated my Tu Fu sessions:
She was as delicate as a butterfly,
    and kindly, very kindly, and ever quiet,
quivering tenderly, or sobbing,
    when I was (often) ugly and untender.

XXX

That never choking—always strangling—sheet, *Imprint*
    dangled a sophomoric politico
from its lines of lawyer-vetted speculation
    and proof-backed "told-ya-so."
Next, Whiz Kid veered into urinal backrooms,
    and got caught living off a Liberal-licensed dole,
granted at aggrieved, taxpayers' expense.
    (Nice to witness Leftist thinking proved right.)
Shortly, my preppy ex-opponent
    found it less possible to become prime minister
than I did to *be* a poet.
    When next I broke with Ontario,
a decade had died since I'd first begun to backtalk—
    i.e., break into print—in hellacious Halifax.

XXXI

Getting back to basics (or just fierce frustration),
    I had to let Y.Z. jet to Hong Kong,
though she really didn't want to "get."
    But I really didn't want to get hitched.
Craved I still Ms. H., her willowy hoodoo.
    But when that woman drove down from Ottawa
to Waterloo, and dished me saltfish and ackee,
    she looked away, distracted, her heart not in it.
Vitiated, I loped to *Europa**—
    red-double-deckered London, red-light-anointed Amsterdam,
red-wine-flooded Paris—
    stripping my bank account in just three weeks.
Dismayed, I sat on a dock on the Seine,
    and wept much and chugged much red wine. Sad to say.

---

*Since 1985, I've shadow-darkened America, Austria, (The) Bahamas, Barbados, Belgium, Bermuda, Brazil, Czech Republic, Cuba, Denmark, Egypt, England, Finland, France, Germany, Gibraltar, Greece, Holland, Hungary, Iceland, Ireland, Italy, Jamaica, Malta, Mauritius, Mexico, Monaco, Morocco, Poland, Portugal, Romania, Russia, Saint-Pierre (et Miquelon), Scotland, Spain, Sweden, Switzerland, Tahiti, Trinidad & Tobago, Turkey, and Zanzibar. Home? Three Mile Plains.

XXXII

Madame H. selected a Sunday School saviour—
    an architect who liked sleepin outdoors
(and so his buildings stayed sketchy).
    Well, I crawled back to HFX and clawed out
a job I couldn't do well—
    social work: driving
rusted-out, busted cars,*
    definitely without a license,
and dropping in on country folk
    to eavesdrop on their speech
for Rock-Steady poems and undulant Soul and what-not.
    I was always ready with incisive ink
to be a holy-roller terror of *Truth*,
    an impeccable imp.

---

*Cf. "Cisshie" and/or "Sock."

XXXIII

Interrogating Highway 1 West,
    Halifax to Weymouth (Falls), I spied
lyric birds music-staff Byzantine apple boughs,
    horses gawk while a train (stabbed by politicians)
limped to its death in a meadow.
    Negro spirits led jamborees in Friday eve barns;
I heard iron-fisted men make steel guitars go crazy,
    make hay of *Music*,
the way a *Kama Sutra* poetess makes love.
    I lived on wind rendered into wine,
breath become bread.
    I composed a Bible (*The Rap*) outta gossip ooze
and neighbourhood drippings—
    the genial muck of Eden.

XXXIV

Lightning could father rainbows, right?
    One night in Digby, rain punctured my brother's roof,
while my voice funneled down an unctuous phone line,
    trying to tunnel into Miz Lady's heart,
but she was laughing, I was flailing.
    "Our" *Love* was truly "lost like lightning" (lb.).
Man, her wrong words hurt my throat
    like I was draining absinthe.
Every maverick thought
    leapt and pulsed with clean blood.
Now, the only rainbows fathered were black ink
    and black vinyl 45s—
dark prisms of spilled gasoline, oozing,
    then catching—like a cold or napalm.

XXXV

Round the Falls—epiphanic, nights brought
    ice cream scooped up nigh a French Shore cathedral
and fully dressed sirens just as sensual
    as undressed nymphs.
(Nay, call them nymphets;
    but imagine nymphos.)
They slaved, gutting fish, but vroomed scarlet roadsters,
    with room only for hugging, kissing, drinking,
simultaneously, yeah.
    What geniuses of *Beauty*!
So sincerely, searingly, unerringly cute,
    acute, cantilevered, frank, they were,
with nudity more naked than any autobiography,
    and infinitely more honest....

XXXVI

Thanks to seven sylphs' audio-visual attractions—
    I mean, their blues, their beauty, their funk, their fire—
Whylah Falls got conceived—maybe—immaculately.
    My inspirations: Liquored-up fits among lilac,
Wilson Pickett bending the ears of a stereo,
    Aretha bending her knees to Marvin Gaye,
and a brown-black WOMAN with a voice like lighter fluid
    and eyes of archetypal lightning—
a Country-n-Western Cleopatra,
    Conway Twitty's very own Diana Ross.
(To find Shelley's like, you gotta be an Egyptologist
    spelunking dark pyramid innards,
then cracking open a gold sarcophagus
    inscribed with Song of Solomon hieroglyphics.)

XXXVII

But despite Shelley's, my, *Love*, unrequited,
    I couldn't quit the notion of *that* hoity-toity dame,
Miz "Ash," sassy temptress, with her cinnamon tresses
    and little tits heightened by tight-tight dresses,
and her epigram telegram haiku letters,
    that I endorsed by acclaiming her "Scintillant Being,"
the Queen of Ecclesiastes.
    And I could too easily get drunk and cry,
cry and drink, slobber tears into my rum,
    already sour, because because because,
ex Halifax, I rode a hard-ass bus seat to court her—
    now a teacher, classy *bourgeoise*, in "Bytown,"
for now I desired her "barefoot and pregnant,"
    but she'd turned Tory—stridin spike heels—so executive.

XXXVIII

Absconding from Clare District, those fantastic Weymouth—
     Whylah—Falls women, their tabloid-typed troubles,
infiltrated I Dal U.'s M.A. refugee-camp.
     Here, I sculpted *Whylah Falls* out of *Lust for Life*
and Monday night symposia with Dr. Fraser*—
     Cambridgian Minnesotan Haligonian—
revising Pound to sound more Mississippian,
     and cranking out a James Brown-debuted
trochaic tetrameter (cranky):
     Yeah, I was tryin to blast open the dam
of ice-clogged, log-jammed, Canuck poesy,
     to repatriate Flanders' fields
to Halifax, to rose-bower the pimp-whipped whores
     circlin and short-circuitin *ye olde* Legislature.

---

*Cf. *Violence in the Arts* (1974).

XXXIX

Professor Fraser was not safe;
    he was a perilous man—
his classes pitched chivalrous, carnival battles—
    M.A. and Ph.D. strivers drivin pencils
and phrases at each other.
    But I was there—
pretendin to be a lover and a boxer.
    I yammered out an essay on Baudelaire—
a.k.a. Bo Diddley—
    his sexing up of *da* alexandrine,
while I hammered LOTS of *Gov.-Gen.* rum,
    tryin to make French mean more than diddly squat.
But that arduous, stammered paper aced
    its A+, eh?

XL

At Dal U.'s Grad House, year-round Valentine's Day,
    played I bone-chillin games of trivia
while tilting toward a buxom, blonde Ukrainian-Can
    and a skinny, brunette German-Can.
Suddenly 27, shooting tequila, I was scared
    to spy a white hair on my head
and to have attained an age, Yeatsian,
    that required quadruple syllables to pronounce.
Due to "runnin on the rent," as Scotian peasants jest,
    I had to hide from Collection Agency goons.
I hied to Gilly's soulful flat, pure rum & purer R & B,
    where *Whylah Falls* kept achin into being.
There, I "got down" with a mocha-sweet bluestocking,
    befo H. McCurdy uplifted me to Parliament.

XLI

Doc McCurdy's summons come just after Y. touched down
     ex-Hong Kong, and off we went,
"A reg'lar couple, *sans* distrust or deep pockets" (Li Po/£),
     skipping from her savings and my $12,000 p.a.,
to Ottawa and my $27,000 per annum,
     and from Halifax to getting hitched—
on October 31, Halloween—it's true—
     and we were supposed to be happy.
Maybe we would've been happy,
     but I kept craving Miss H., now suavely bureaucratic,
and we parlayed whispers into secret rendezvous.
     Then I'd slouch to my couch and play Sixties Soul,
howling, growling, in harmony, hoping,
     and harming, marring, my marriage until....

XLII

Those Centre Block, House of "Corrections" years
    mandated slapstick Opposition. I loved
carolling true blues—uninhibited Hansard—
    from our upstairs office downstairs to editors,
to set free McCurdy's speeches, cadenced
    for *History* and "the Canadian people."
Glorious it was to kick back on Fridays,
    uncork *Ballantine's* Scotch and unfurl *The Globe and Mail*,
and curse out Mulroney, slushy Mulroney, sleazy Mulroney,
    or, gratefully, to chow down
in the plush-to-the-tush Parliamentary Restaurant.
    But my downscale digs down Byward Market
saw grungy harlots stoop fast on our doorstep,
    humongous rats troop fast through our cupboards.

XLIII

Alas, some days it was culpably cold, even in April,
    and my spouse, Y.Z., was righteously unhappy.
And I was not very happy.

    But I finished (window) dressing *Whylah Falls*:
I had hauled it out of Weymouth Falls' kitchens,
    Gilly's flat, J. Fraser's living room,
and McCurdy's office—
    like a disciple of *Love*,
undisciplined *Love*.

    Whylah Falls was a brick launched through library stained glass,
and scholars went at it like a lost blues score.

    Nothing mediocre—no tin-pan Opry—found there.
Something "un-Canadian," hissed a critic.

    Si, it snagged Ottawa's Archie Lampman laurels.

XLIV

Unceremoniously, Y. skipped the glitzy ceremony.
  I attracted an attractive translator
who'd just abandoned, had to abandon, Parliament Hill:
  We had transcended that bastion of *Morality*.
Luncheons, suppers, postcards, and letters later
  (while Y. was estranged, cramming in Library Science),
brought I into the breach of *petit* treason.
  I can't talk about it. I'm impeachable.
But the embraces continued and concretized,
  coalescing a mirror-marriage.
Consequently, in my second-year Ph.D. at Queen's,
  I packed Y.Z. off to T.O., weeping, weeping.
Mutually. (Where is she now?
  I'd like to see her. She was my wife.)

XLV

While *Whylah* slurped a cascade of honey reviews,
    dulcet reviews, I managed to imagine
Fire on the Water: An Anthology of Black Nova Scotian Writing,
    and soon it dawned (in *two* volumes, no less).
Suddenly, Duke U., #1 in slam dunks and Deconstruction,
    summoned lil ol me,
shocking every Queen's English speaker at Queen's,
    even though my dissertation interbreeding
snowy Canuck and inky Yank poesy
    was sworn out in four sweltering June weeks,
in the graduate Rez of Kingston, ON (& on *ad nauseam*).
    In the street, rednecks in a black muscle car
screamed "Niggerrrrr!" at me one late black midnight
    when I was lugging groceries, my black hands full.

XLVI

Down rocketed I from Queen to Duke,
    down to Durham, No'th Car'lina,
like a bat out of a blizzard,
    seeking magnolia for shelter.
I became a guerilla of monographs,
    haulin the heaviest, most devious dictionaries,
sweatin out my eyes,
    with my Afro gone real natchal picky.
Now I stood on ancestral soil,
    the homeland, South, funky Dixie:
How could I not okay "our patriotic," cruise missile kills?
    Clintonian America was plumb sexy,
and its uglified, fecal enemies had to breathe worms.
    Then, the Divorce decree sprung me, unhinged me....

XLVII

Taught I like a Jesse / James / Brown impersonator,
    chalkin up screechin, blackboard climaxes,
positin post-structuralist agitation,
    XXX cogitation, pseudo-psycho upset,
you know, doin it.
    And I motored those tobacco-sweetened streets
in a black rag-top, 1990, white *Miata*
    some black-haired white girl titled "Yoko Ono."
That *traductrice* who helped mother *Lush Dreams, Blue Exile,*
    was still "mine," still in Canada;
still I sued elastically hard-to-get others—
    Canuck chicks gone sultry mong *da* Tarheels.
Then Jimmy Rolfe writ, "Jimmy me a libretto?"
    My brain twitched orncry and gruesome....

XLVIII

Sought I to type over the poet Shelley
    in fealty to the Supreme Shelley—
that cinnamon-and-pepper saint of *Whylah Falls*—
    but with a value-added, Charles Bukowski accent.
So I plunked an Italian Renaissance, bloody incest tale
    in a slave-labour, Nova Scotian apple orchard.
Thus, *Beatrice Chancy* sprouted in Durham,
    out of a dismal apartment,
daily duels with cockroaches,
    and gouts of red wine kept chilled in the fridge
(to garnish heated readings of Dante's *Inferno*).
    I jetted *gialli* and sweated jet,
raking sacredly naked, Taschen pictorials,
    or staking my heart on passion-pit teases.

XLIX

While I aided and abetted the apparition
    of *Beatrice Chancy*, opera and play,
and handcrafted a movie picturing, but not depicting, *Whylah Falls*—
    Virgo's *One Heart Broken Into Song* (1999)—
my one-and-only, one-and-only, my only-one Mom,
    was dwindling away, vertigo pon vertigo.
But amid her passive—yet aggressive—decline,
    she recollected two dissected cousins.
I had to dig up each cadaver outta Archives,
    restore each, gaudy, to front-page news.
George and Rufus Hamilton demanded a long poem—
    a novel—in which to be sumptuously shown,
to cleanse the criminal grime from their bones:
    No whitewash, just light.

L

Still dandy and scholarly in Durham,
    All-American City, Tree City, City of Medicine, U.S.A.,
I set to carvin out the nastiest lines—
    grisly, bleeding cuts of live meat.
I had to savour *Liberty* in the Great Republic,
    to yowl whatever the hell I wanted.
Still I shunted endlessly to Ottawa,
    and back again, and still numbered—hand-lettered—
that movie, essays, a libretto, and two plays,
    all anointed by the N.S. Government's
$25,000 Portia White Prize (yahoo, y'all)
    and then a Rockefeller (N.Y.C.) Fellowship.
Now I could polish *Beatrice Chancy* in Bellagio,
    and plot *Whylah Falls* as black humour while tippling *negron.*

LI

My belovèd daughter, Aurélia, was born—
    Wondrous Treasure,
warm, breathing, living Gold—
    Incontrovertibly precious,
and I was suddenly a true peer,
    I mean, *"père"*—
and subsequently (nowadays) "Pup."
    A.M.-C. is right honourable:
I pray she will be happy all of her days,
    avoid all my sore errors (*et cetera*),
be as ingenious and wise and kind
    as she is beautiful, mindful, and cheerful,
and find good fortune in *Art*,
    and even better fortune in *Life*.

LII

Canting after a sirocco—a *mirage*—ex-Mauritius—
    after a month in Italy and seven at McGill—
I fell also under the spell of the U. of T.
    Now, *Beatrice Chancy* incarnated—vivacious,
glamorous, lethal, showcasing diva "Measha B.,"
    and then the instantly sold-out book broke out,
pursuant to *Whylah Falls: The Play.*
    Shortly, its players tread Ottawa boards,
scoring 97% attendance (pretty popular),
    but plaguing killjoys.
So? I kept chopping up bloody poems into hunks
    of *Malice*, strips of *Beauty*—
the Frankenstein formula for *Blue.*
    Next stop: N.B.—to pry open The Celestial City's Gaol!

LIII

I had to spy where George and Rufus got swung
    from a rope—as if in Hitchcock-like child's play.
Back in "Tea.Dot," I exhumed *Execution Poems*—
    Gothic, darkling lyrics that denied nothing
except well-schooled, well-tooled English.
    They were prepared with libertine liquor,
turpentine *Clarity*, serpentine *Wit*.
    Entering them, you stumble into
an abyss of Cajun, deep-fried blues—
    an Africadian accent black at bottom.
Their lines are as jagged as a D-Day beach.
    Their ink is no medicine.
I couldn't use any post-modernist logic.
    My duty? To be as graphic as a crucifix.

LIV

Then Mom slept away, passing on at home—
    several family at her bedside,
a priceless, rare miracle, in our day,
    when most of us decease, rotting in nursing homes,
or alone in hospitals, our pricey plugs pulled.
    Yet died she a too-young 61.
Alienated, we wept, but bore this inalienable curse,
    just as we bore Nona's *fin-de-siècle* suicide,
just as we too-soon bore her singular brother's casket
    to Maplewood Cemetery in Windsor, N.S.
I bought four burial plots—
    my first real-estate purchase—
and then I purchased my mother's land,
    3/4–acre, up home, in Three Mile Plains.

LV

Once M.I.A., *Madelle* H. unveiled next her pert face
    when *One Heart Broken Into Song* silvered
The National Library screen.
    "Mrs. Dr." dismissed my succubus as "insignificant"
and "mousy," and I knew Rehab:
    Hankering at last halted.
In dreams back in the 80s,
    I'd be gripping that spectral entertainment,
when she'd peel free her bod, then, flippant, slip off,
    and I'd awake, sodden.
If only I'd read *In Praise of Older Women* sooner,
    I'd've panted fewer, faint-hearted albas,
I'd've been less hallucinatory.
    I'd've sunk more spunk into my sonnets.

LVI

Execution Poems was this big, black book.
    Blood-hued acid was the titular ink.
Readily, the poems, dramatically erratic,
    strayed into the epic of a novel.
(*George & Rue* could not emerge yet, however,
    from Bellagio and the Hotel Vancouver.)
But *Blue* edged along, consciously atrociously too—
    using a jigsaw poetry, a hacksaw poetry,
to maim critics with one eye already gouged out,
    mangle those already on Death Row.
Surprise! *Execution Poems* set me face-to-face
    with Her Excellency The Governor-General of Canada,
The Right Honourable Adrienne Clarkson,
    who delivered me the poison-pen prize.

LVII

Right after 11/09/01 got struck from the calendars,
    Ajay Heble phoned in a commission
for a Guelph Jazz Fest opera, of all things,
    and d-d Jackson of N.Y.C. and I
immediately conjured *Québécité*,
    and put it in the offing,
to float high-minded, but big-assed sounds,
    a multicultural callaloo
of symphonic Rhythm-n-Blues, Indo alap, Korean scat,
    trash-talk English, *et pissoir* French,
to urge audiences whoop and cheer
    and kick dullards back on their fat, fartin duffs.
When this opera shoutin *Love* rocked Jazz,
    Downbeat squawked bout "tragically hijacked Québécois symbols."

LVIII

No, just cymbals, maybe.
     But extravaganza flared, rainbow-proud,
unapologetic, Bollywood fanfare blaring.
     Everyone who hears it hears Miles Davis
debatin with Delibes and Juliette Gréco,
     or John Coltrane odysseying through India,
or *Les Parapluies de Cherbourg*, but with rain
     imported from Vancouver and Hong Kong.
But now I dug down to lift up *George & Rue*,
     a blood-soaked, tear-soaked book,
to thaw out frigid consciences
     by re-staging two festive hangings.
(The more I hung round the Hamilton bros,
     the more resembled they Shakespeare's Aaron[*].)

---

[*]Cf. Titus Andronicus.

LIX

Accidentally, I've here blacked out some passages—
    those nights lounging in strangers' rooms,
barfing concoctions of sugar cookies and plonk,
    after hours fixin liquored pals' tricky lyrics,
deciding what was imperishably publishable,
    what wasn't,
cutting through cobwebs of adjectives
    to free the startling, tarantula verbs.
On my birthday and on New Year's Day,
    I liked—like—to ogle lake, river, or ocean.
Every April-*Nisan*, May, June,
    I must eye apple blossoms.
Spot these eccentricities—oddities—in *Gold Indigoes*,
    Eyeing the North Star, and even *Odysseys Home* (essays).

LX

Sprung from the House of "Comix"
    (in prissy, fussbudget Ottawa)—
then released from the U.S. "Arms"—
    brassy, brass-knuckle America—
and lured from Duke U., post-McGill—
    and now rusticating in T.O., this Big Crab Apple,
this wanna-be, instantly has-been Manhattan,
    with my garden of weeds and raspberries,
my fruitful vineyard (raccoon-compromised),
    plus peaches (sometimes) and lilacs in May,
I am poor husband to an extraordinary wife,
    who is so deeply, clearly good,
whose every sentence is an aphorism,
    and who makes *Perfection* her *Art*.

LXI

Still a bard of backtalk—or "extremist" exuberance—
    and *Vice* worked with gusto,
I look back, tonight, Canada Day, 2005,
    thirty years after having begun,
in Halifax again, where I am right now,
    with the *Blessing* who is my daughter, A.M.-C.
While fireworks light up the dark harbour,
    I marvel at the P.E. Trudeau Fellowship Prize,
plus U. of T. tenure—or immunity from prosecution,
    plus *Health* still holding (letting me hold onto *Love*),
and I gotta admit, I gotta say,
    "It is good....
'*I feel good....*'*
    Sorry for all my ill deeds."

---

*Cf. Brown (1965).

CODA: 1/12/13

Beauty for beauty....
        —ANNA MINERVA HENDERSON

LXII

854 lines captured in one day:
    61 "Rap Sonnets"* raptured in one day—
July 1, 2005—to laud July 1, 1975,
    my esoteric assent to *making*.
All that water under Macdonald Bridge since,
    and under Longfellow Bridge now,
must be anti-climactic or antediluvian.
    On that long holiday of drafting,
I was serving my second marriage.
    Last March, I got handed my third bachelorhood—
a timing that crosses this thirteenth collection:
    Traverse.
(Jeez, just last week, it was still titled,
    "Thirty Years [1975-2005].")

---

*Rhapsodic sonnets.

LXIII

Thirty years it still is now,
    since 1983 and the starter book.
Too black in heart, I've been smart at treachery
    (*Lechery*), though my tax returns
aspire to *Righteousness*: Nothing less!
    And I do weep for my wrongs:
If this will make anyone like me more,
    I confess I've lost much since "Oh-5."
I scribed "Thirty Years"—and 61 days later
    my Dad was dead,
impossibly: I couldn't imagine
    he was no more, that no more
could I argue against him,
    or say that I loved awful him awfully.

LXIV

Morphine-delirious, he'd hollered for me,
    out his hospital bed, but I was gone,
far off to Finland (for the first time)
    and next to *Auld* Scotland,
and so I landed in Canada to whiplashing alarms:
    "Your father's in the hospital."
(*Can't be!*)
    I dialed his Doc who popped me an opiate:
Hope. "You got time." Nope: An hour later,
    Bill Clarke, 70, was deceased.
I jetted, YYZ to YHZ, wet-faced irrefutably.
    Called I Alexa McDonough, M.P.,
ex-*Kindergarten* teacher (mine), asked,
    "Could you arrange a burial plot for W.L. Clarke?"

LXV

She did. He lies in Fairview Cemetery,
    nigh the *Titanic* drowned
and Halifax Explosion crushed.
    Flabbergasted were the gravediggers:
"An M.P. called and demanded
    that we open a space.
We had to make one. The cemetery is closed."
    But there really is no space
to hold that man's conversation.
    In our last talks, he bashed the bankers ("bandits"),
and I mentioned I'd been to Dealey Plaza
    and saw where *Camelot* came apart,
and how paltry is the site—
    despite its majesty in mythology.

LXVI

His will was his *Diary 1959*:
    "For George, so he will understand."
May '59: His paternity germinating,
    I unfolded in ma mama's womb.
But he was in love with a different woman,
    and was loving different women—
a Zen praxis his motorcycle finessed—
    from Halifax to Harlem to Hochelaga.
Also, his railway job let him "make tracks"—
    to skip to Moncton once romances mouldered,
and put away the purple *B.M.W.* and pick up paints
    and make good art and take good money.
But, once born, I was dying; so Grammy telegrammed,
    "Come see your son before he's dead."

LXVII

If my lusts look "predatory,"
    it's hereditary,
right? "That's no excuse," say mad, sad mates.
    No, but it's an explanation,
though no *Expiation*,
    to plead, "I am my father's son."
I cracked the *Diary*:
    Drafting that unending novel, "The Motorcyclist,"
Bill's psyche got transplanted right into my head.
    My craft brought me then to drafty Rhodes—
orange-blossom, lemon-fragrant Rodos—
    isle of colossal winds, rock-smacking seas—
lip-smacking ouzo, and a Nordic belle—
    Sixties sun-goddess—not one iota platonic.

LXVIII

We plucked shells from blue surf by Durrell's house.
　　Round back, mong the Muslim headstones,
she split part a eucalyptus pip
　　and bid me smell. *Love* fired up, pungent.
Her hair? Red flame. Her eyes? Mediterranean cerulean.
　　I couldn't profess my feeling. Not then.
I oppressed myself, pressed myself to work:
　　Trudeau: Long March / Shining Path blazed
a way to now praise Bill Clarke, proletarian artist.
　　Whylah Falls got rendered in Mandarin,
thus acquiring Cathay cachet. Another title roared
　　out in Romanian, and brought me lira
non-negotiable, plus a bronze statuette
　　I winged home: Academy award.

LXIX

I should list here *I & I*, a verse-novel
    as pulp-fiction, ballpointedly penned—
as a teen, pointedly, when I was criminally innocent of *Art*....
    Illuminated Verses discloses ebon nudes—
women lookin sharp, or well-rounded,
    thus disconcerting closet, Canuckistan Puritans.
Jon Paul Fiorentino felt his way through *Blues and Bliss*—
    Selected Poems—to collect the Hoffer Prize.
2010: *Whylah Falls* came garbed in a Third Edition,
    and *Blue*—and *Black*—each got a Second Edition.
April 2011: *Red* blushed onto newsstands.
    That same spring, I exited the marital abode,
elected exile to the Upper, Upper Beaches,
    and wrought a home with—at last—room for my child.

LXX

An Ivory Tower Black, I gotta ink, chalk up, essays:
    So, *Directions Home* delineates Africadians.
But an overseas elderessa oversees *Illicit Sonnets*
    (that *The* [London] *Guardian* approves—
as an *apéritif* to Ed Snowden's heady confessions).
    Venezia issued my verses in Montale's tongue*,
and so I've enjoyed quaffin a lot of *Punt e Mes*.
    Lasso the Wind: Aurélia's Verses and Other Poems
is fresh out, children's lyrics crooned by a Harvard Prof
    (just visiting), but also the Poet Laureate of Toronto
(appointed under a mayor admittedly prone to crack).
    I'll pause here: I pray for increase of *Love*—
and for flourishing *Health* and for nourishing *Art*.
    But Ecclesiastes 12 owns the last word.

---

*Cf. Joseph Pivato, ed., *Africadian Atlantic* (2012).

COLOPHONIC

I think beauty should be circulated.

—REID KENNETH WHITE[*]

[*]Cf. John DeMont, "'Scrummager' shares sunshine," *The Chronicle-Herald* (Halifax, N.S., 30/11/13.)

CROSSING (OVER)

Hero incognito? That's Mr. C.P.Z.,
    he of the "Pound-plain poems" whose edits
better other poets,
     especially I. When—If—I score plaudits,
they're echoes of his protocols in poetics,
    the provisos of his verses, always best.
My ally and comrade now for thirty years,
    Choucri Paul Zemokhol also advises poets
to treasure fonts—their tenor and tone.
    Thus, I point out that Exile has typeset *Traverse*[*]
in Bodoni SvtyTwo, Constantia, Cochin and Trajan fonts,
    and I thank the two Callaghans, Barry and son Michael,
for impressing this book, with requisite art.
    Whatever here be maladroit betrays my hand.

---

[*]The work was writ in Halifax, Nova Scotia, in 2005 and in Cambridge, Massachusetts, in 2013. It was edited in Cambridge (MA), Zurich (Switzerland), and in Ottawa and Toronto (Ontario), with the stringent assistance of Mr. C.P.Z., who is, as usual, blameless for infelicities in style and/or inaccuracies in story. Cf. "The Revelationist Manifesto."

George Elliott Clarke's many honours include the Portia White Prize for Artistic Achievement (1998), Governor General's Award for Poetry (2001), National Magazine Gold Medal for Poetry (2001), Dr. Martin Luther King Jr. Achievement Award (2004), Pierre Elliott Trudeau Fellowship Prize (2005-2008), Dartmouth Book Award for Fiction (2006), Poesis Premiul (2006, Romania), Eric Hoffer Book Award for Poetry (2009), appointment to the Order of Nova Scotia (2006), appointment to the Order of Canada at the rank of Officer (2008), and eight honorary doctorates. He is a pioneering scholar of African-Canadian literature and is the E.J. Pratt Professor of Canadian Literature at the University of Toronto, having previously held posts at Duke University and McGill University. With poetry translated into books in Romania (2006), China (2006), and Italy (2012), Clarke was appointed a Visiting Professor at Harvard University (2013-14) and Poet Laureate of Toronto (2012-15).